Rob Le~~

Mr Dunfilling
and the
Toothy Monster

SIMON & SCHUSTER
YOUNG BOOKS

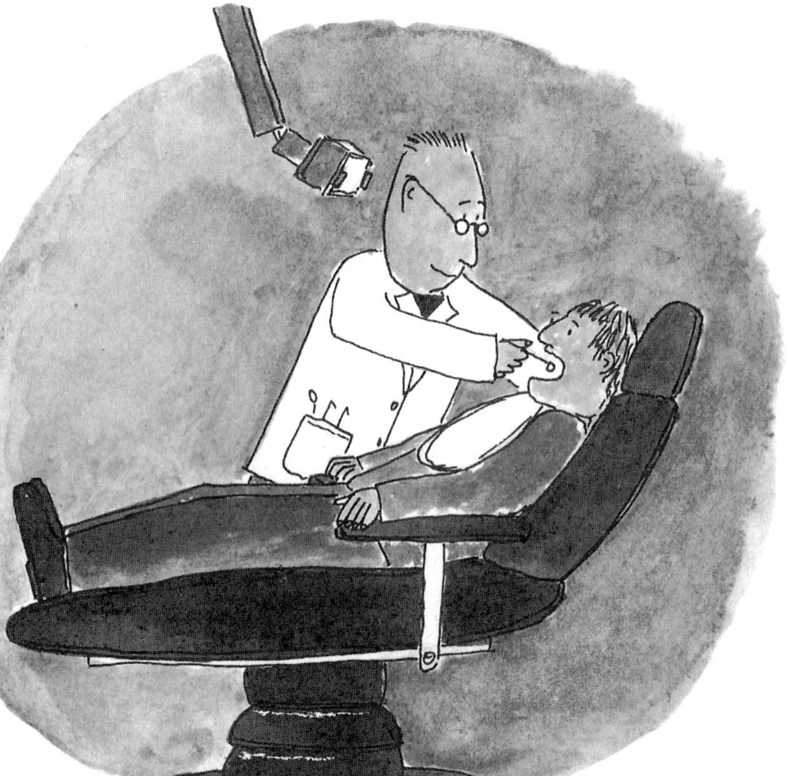

1. The Telephone Call

Mr Dunfilling was a brilliant dentist. There wasn't a tooth that he couldn't fill.

He had little round glasses and a very high forehead with a little tuft of hair on top. People who knew him said he had a high forehead because of his brains. He was certainly very clever. He had lots of important letters after his name but he never boasted about them.

If Dunfilling had one fault it was that he couldn't say "no". He would accept every patient to his surgery, no matter how hard the job was.

But one Wednesday morning he had a very unusual telephone call. It was to be his hardest job ever.

"It's Mr Cage, the zookeeper," said his receptionist.

Mr Dunfilling picked up the telephone and asked what the matter was. "Has one of your monkeys dropped your false teeth down the toilet again?"

"No, nothing like that," laughed the zookeper. "One of my animals has toothache and won't eat because of the pain. Can you fix it?"

"Of course," said Mr Dunfilling. "My receptionist will make you an appointment."

At lunchtime Mrs Trimble, the receptionist, tottered into the surgery. "Mr Cage is coming next Tuesday at two-thirty," she said.

"Fine," said Mr Dunfilling.

Mrs Trimble was a very nervous old lady and he could hear her false teeth rattling around in her mouth.

"Whatever is the matter?" asked Mr Dunfilling.

"Dear oh deary me. There's something that Mr Cage didn't tell you," she said, sounding worried. "This animal has ten thousand teeth!"

"What?" he said, sitting down with a shock.

Then he got another shock and stood up again. He had sat down on his drill.

"Ten thousand teeth! How will I find the right tooth?"

"Oh dear oh deary me. I suppose you'll just have to take lots of X-rays," suggested Mrs Trimble.

"Hmmm," said Mr Dunfilling thoughtfully. "You had better keep Tuesday afternoon free of appointments. I think this job will take a long time."

When Mr Dunfilling was lying in bed that night he began to think about what the animal might be like. Ten thousand teeth was a lot of teeth. An animal would have to have a very large mouth to fit that number of teeth inside.

Mr Dunfilling gulped. Where there was a large mouth there would be a large head, and where there was a large head there would be a large body – and a large everything else.

Could it be a big guard dog? he wondered. Or perhaps a lion? But lions and dogs couldn't have more than about fifty teeth.

He began to think of fierce Nile crocodiles, but even they didn't have ten thousand teeth.

What about sharks? They had lots of sharp teeth. This animal must be *really* big. Could it be a whale?

Surely Mr Cage couldn't bring a whale, and the water for it to swim in, to his surgery. He'd have to work under water as well.

What about a dragon? But no, he didn't think that dragons really existed. Or did they?

If the animal had toothache it would be in a very bad mood. It might go wild and smash up his surgery. All his expensive equipment would be ruined. And how would he give the creature an injection to make it sleep? He didn't like the idea of reaching into the creature's mouth while it was still awake.

He also remembered that the creature hadn't eaten for some time because of the bad tooth. By next Tuesday it would be starving!

"When that creature wakes up from the anaesthetic, the first meal it will see will be a dentist!" he thought.

While Mr Dunfilling was asleep, his extra large brain gave him extra large nightmares about huge toothy monsters.

2. Mr Dunfilling Prepares

When Mr Dunfilling woke up the next morning he was still worried about the creature. He'd almost decided to telephone Mr Cage and tell him that he couldn't deal with the tooth.

But then he changed his mind. He couldn't let a poor animal suffer with painful toothache.

"What can I do?" he said to Mrs Trimble when he arrived at work. "This surgery isn't built for huge creatures with ten thousand teeth."

"Never mind about your surgery, what about me, Mr Dunfilling? I shall be eaten alive!" she said shakily.

Mr Dunfilling looked her up and down. She was as thin and knobbly as a stick. He didn't think the creature would find her very appetising.

Mrs Trimble trembled. "I was wondering if I might have Tuesday afternoon off because my grandmother is very ill."

"Of course you may," said Mr Dunfilling, although he found it difficult to believe that old Mrs Trimble could still have a grandmother alive.

By lunchtime, Mr Dunfilling's great mind had thought of a plan. He made a list of the things he would need and then he set off to do some shopping. The first place he visited was the costume shop where he hired a suit of armour.

"Going to a fancy dress party are you, sir?" asked the shopkeeper.

"Er . . . yes, that's right," said Mr Dunfilling. He couldn't tell the man that it was really to protect him from being eaten by a creature with ten thousand teeth. The news would have been all around the town by the end of the day. Mr Dunfilling hoped he wouldn't have to return the armour full of dents!

The next place he visited was the scrap yard where he bought some car doors and bonnets.

At the tool shop he bought some nuts and bolts and a blow torch.

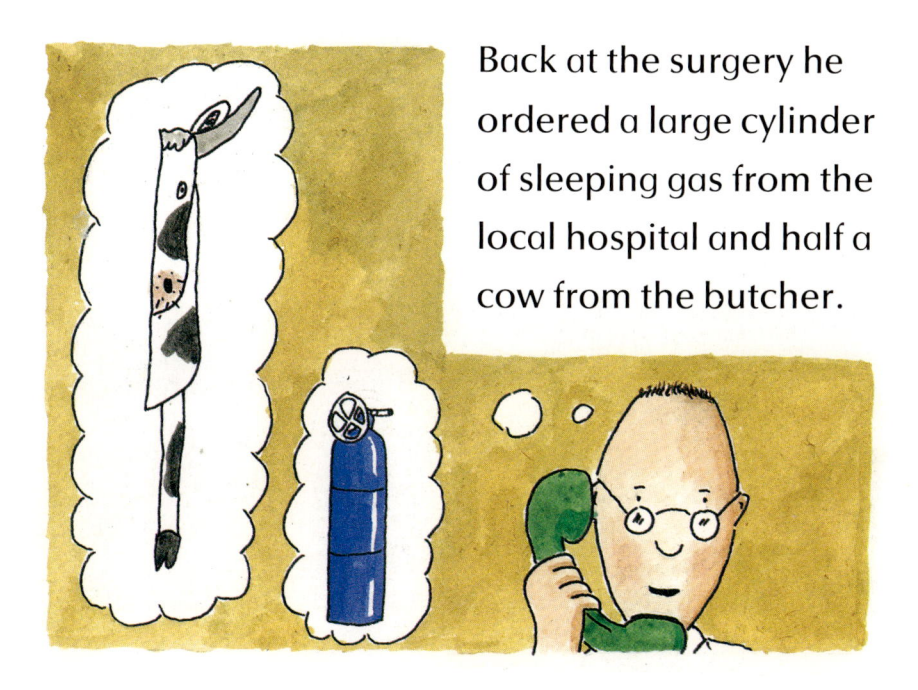

Finally he called at the camping shop and bought the largest tent they had.

Back at the surgery he ordered a large cylinder of sleeping gas from the local hospital and half a cow from the butcher.

Over the next few evenings Mr Dunfilling welded the car doors and bonnets to the floor, ceiling and walls of his surgery using the blow torch. Then he bolted all his expensive equipment to the floor. He had now made the surgery safe in case the creature went wild.

He hung the tent from the ceiling. He planned to drop the tent over the creature and fill it with gas until the animal was asleep.

With great difficulty he managed to cram half a cow into his freezer (though the legs stuck out), which he planned to give the creature as a snack when it woke up.

He knocked down a few walls so that the creature could get up the stairs, and lastly he tried on his suit of armour. It fitted perfectly.

3. The News Spreads

Staying with Mrs Trimble that week was her grandson, Ricky. He overheard his grandmother telling her next door neighbour about Mr Dunfilling and the creature. Ricky was fascinated by monsters and dinosaurs. It would be wonderful to see a real one!

"Can I help Mr Dunfilling with the toothy monster on Tuesday?" he asked his grandmother.

"Oh deary me, I don't know. Won't you be frightened?" she said.

"No, not a bit. Please can you ask Mr Dunfilling?" he pleaded.

"Well, I suppose he'll look after you. He's a very sensible man. Make sure you don't get in his way." She telephoned Mr Dunfilling. He was very happy to have Ricky along to help.

Meanwhile, Mrs Trimble's neighbour told everyone at Clodhoppers Shoe Factory, where she worked, about the creature. They told the workers at Noddles Hat Factory during a factory workers' party, and so the news spread until the story reached the ears of Stan Meddler, the sharpest reporter at the *Daily Smudge*.

That evening, after Mr Dunfilling had gone home, Stan sneaked round to the back of the surgery. He had with him his ultra-expandable, superduper periscopic ladder, eight expensive cameras and lots of zoom lenses. He pressed a button on the ultra-expandable, superduper periscopic ladder and it shot up the wall. He

26

climbed up to the window and peered in.

He saw the metal-lined walls, the widened doorway, the tent hanging from the ceiling and all Mr Dunfilling's equipment bolted to the floor.

"It's true!" he gasped and fell off his ladder into the dustbins of Greasioni's Restaurant. "What a story this will make!"

Stan hurried back to his office. It would be front page news tomorrow morning. The headline would be *"Daring Dentist Defies Death from Dangerous Dinosaur!"* – or better still *"MAN MENDS MONSTER'S MUNCHERS!"*

He sat down excitedly and started to write the story.

"Good gracious and good grief!" said Mrs Smithington-Smythe picking up the morning newspaper from a silver tray. "Dentists treating *animals* – how disgusting!"

Mrs Smithington-Smythe wasn't worried about the fact that, according to the newspaper, the creature had ten thousand teeth and was probably ten metres tall with smoke coming from its nostrils. This was because she was a very fierce lady herself. (Some unkind people might have said that she was more than a match for the creature.)

29

If there was one thing that was guaranteed to make Mrs Smithing-Smythe explode with anger, it was uncleanliness. She was the sort of person who insisted that all her plates, cups, knives and forks were washed at least ten times and she used a magnifying glass to inspect them for smears.

The news about Mr Dunfilling made her so

angry that the veins in her neck started bulging and she began to shake.

"All those clean, sterilized instruments in that creature's revolting mouth! And it will be dribbling all over the floor! IT'S GOT TO STOP!" she roared, stabbing a potato with her fork and squirting the maid with butter. "Bring me the telephone. I will talk to the mayor at once!"

The mayor said there was nothing he could do. There was no law against dentists treating animal teeth as long as they had passed the right exams – and he was sure Mr Dunfilling had.

"In that case I will organize a protest!" bellowed Mrs Smithington-Smythe.

The mayor held the telephone away from his ear so that he wouldn't be deafened and said, "But I've heard this animal has ten thousand teeth and is ten metres tall. Won't people be afraid to turn up to a protest?"

"Pah!" said Mrs Smithington-Smythe. "When I lived in Africa I swatted *flies* bigger than that!" She slammed down the telephone and then began ringing all her friends.

Everyone agreed to come because they were a bit afraid of Mrs Smithington-Smythe. Secretly they thought that Mr Dunfilling was very brave to be treating such a fierce animal.

4. The Creature Comes to Town

On Tuesday morning the town was empty. People had boarded up their shops and houses just in case the creature got loose.

The only people not safely hidden away in their houses were the ones in the crowd outside Mr Dunfilling's surgery. In front of them stood Mrs Smithington-Smythe brandishing a placard saying "CREATURE GO HOME". Other banners said "NO DIRTY DENTISTS HERE" and "DENTISTS FOR HUMANS ONLY".

Mr Dunfilling, wearing his suit of armour and with Ricky by his side, watched the crowd from his surgery window. They were both very nervous.

"Now Ricky," said Mr Dunfilling, "when the creature arrives, you must hide in the toilet until it is safely asleep. Then you can watch me work and hand me my instruments."

In the distance a lorry appeared. The crowd went very quiet. They could see huge puffs of black smoke coming from the back of the lorry. As it came nearer they could also hear a terrifying roar.

Although the crowd was frightened of Mrs Smithington-Smythe, by now they were much more frightened of the creature in the back of the zookeeper's van. They quickly fled for the safety of their houses.

Mrs Smithington-Smythe, seeing that she was suddenly alone, stormed off back to her mansion in disgust.

The zoo lorry came to a halt outside Mr Dunfilling's surgery and Mr Cage jumped out. He went to ring the door bell but Mr Dunfilling had already opened the door, so he rang the dentist's nose by mistake.

"Hello," said Mr Cage, looking Mr Dunfilling up and down. "I'll just get the animal out of the back of the lorry."

Mr Dunfilling watched nervously as Mr Cage unlocked the doors and climbed into the back of the lorry.

There was a clumping, clamping sound. Was that the creature or just the zookeeper's feet? Mr Cage jumped down from the back of the lorry carrying a small box.

Peering through the window in the toilet door, Ricky watched as Mr Cage carried the box up the widened stairs and into the surgery. Mr Dunfilling clanked and creaked cautiously behind him.

"It must be the creature's lunch," Mr Dunfilling thought, although it didn't seem much to get ten thousand teeth into. It was just as well that he had half a cow in the freezer.

Mr Cage lifted the lid.

"Here's your patient," he said.

Sitting on a small tray in the middle of the box was a large snail.

"It's a rare tropical snail from Mullawullaland," Mr Cage added, proudly.

He looked around at the metal-lined walls of the surgery and saw all the equipment bolted to the floor and the tent hanging from the ceiling.

Then he realized Mr Dunfilling's misunderstanding and a big grin appeared on his face. "You were expecting a huge animal weren't you?" he chuckled.

"Er . . . yes, I was," said Mr Dunfilling, feeling rather silly.

Then the dentist smiled. "Come on out, Ricky! Meet the creature with ten thousand teeth!"

Ricky crept cautiously into the surgery. He was very surprised to see the snail.

"I'm sorry," said the zookeeper to Mr Dunfilling. "I should have told you on the telephone. Snails have ten thousand tiny teeth. They're called cuticles."

"Oh, I see!" said Mr Dunfilling, hastily climbing out of his armour.

"Don't worry. I won't tell anyone," smiled Mr Cage.

43

After a quick burst of sleeping gas the snail was snoring softly.

Mr Dunfilling found the bad tooth on the tiny X-ray, and then Ricky held the magnifying glass while Mr Dunfilling looked into the snail's tiny mouth. The tooth was too small to fill, so Mr Dunfilling plucked it out with a tiny pair of tweezers.

The snail didn't feel a thing.

Mr Cage thanked Mr Dunfilling and Ricky, and drove off with the happy snail.

"Mr Cage must get the exhaust pipe on his lorry fixed," thought Mr Dunfilling. "It's pouring out clouds of black smoke and making a terrible noise."

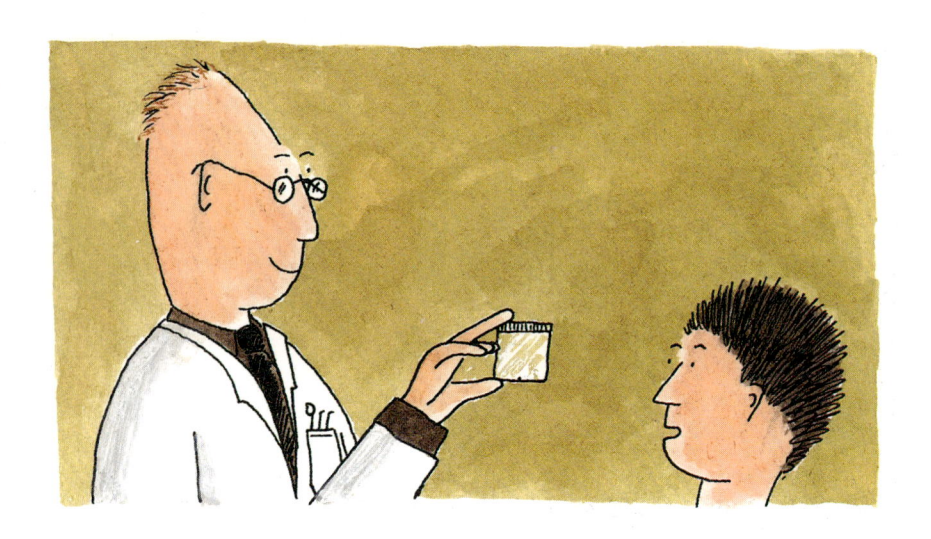

Then he turned to Ricky and handed him a little glass jar with a tiny tooth inside. "Here's a little souvenir," he said.

"Wow!" said Ricky.

"Don't forget. You must keep it a secret."

The people of the town, hiding in their houses, never did find out the truth. Mrs Smithington-Smythe wrote lots of letters to the *Daily Smudge* about dirty animals at the dentist, but nobody took any notice.

They all thought Mr Dunfilling was the bravest dentist alive, and his appointment book was always full.